Empty Nest

CAROL ANN DUFFY lives in Manchester, where she is Professor and Creative Director of the Writing School at Manchester Metropolitan University. She has written for both children and adults, and her poetry has received many awards, including the Signal Prize for Children's Verse, the Whitbread, Forward and T. S. Eliot Prizes, and the Lannan and E. M. Forster Prize in America. She was appointed Poet Laureate in 2009. In 2011 *The Bees* won the Costa Poetry Award, and in 2012 she won the PEN Pinter Prize. She was appointed DBE in 2015.

Also by Carol Ann Duffy in Picador

Standing Female Nude
Selling Manhattan
The Other Country
Mean Time
The World's Wife
Feminine Gospels
New Selected Poems
Rapture
Mrs Scrooge
Love Poems
Another Night Before Christmas
The Bees
The Christmas Truce
Wenceslas
Bethlehem
Ritual Lighting
Dorothy Wordsworth's Christmas Birthday
Collected Poems
The Wren-Boys
The King of Christmas
Pablo Picasso's Noël
Frost Fair
Sincerity

AS EDITOR
Hand in Hand
Answering Back
To the Moon
Off the Shelf

Empty Nest

Poems for Families

EDITED BY
CAROL
ANN
DUFFY

PICADOR

First published 2021 by Picador
an imprint of Pan Macmillan
6 Briset Street, London ECIM 5NR
EU representative: Macmillan Publishers Ireland Limited,
Mallard Lodge, Lansdowne Village, Dublin 4
Associated companies throughout the world
www.panmacmillan.com

ISBN 978-1-5290-2868-3

1 3 5 7 9 8 6 4 2

A CIP catalogue record for this book is available from the British Library.

Printed and bound by CPI Group (UK) Ltd, Croydon, CR0 4YY

Visit **www.picador.com** to read more about all our books
and to buy them. You will also find features, author interviews and
news of any author events, and you can sign up for e-newsletters
so that you're always first to hear about our new releases.

Contents

Empty Nest

Autumn Birds

The wild duck startles like a sudden thought
And heron slow as if it might be caught.
The flopping crows on weary wings go by
And grey beard jackdaws noising as they fly.
The crowds of starnels wiz and hurry by
And darken like a cloud the evening sky.
The larks like thunder rise and study round
Then drop and nestle in the stubble ground.
The wild swan hurries high and noises loud
With white necks peering to the evening cloud.
The weary rooks to distant woods are gone;
With length of tail the magpie winnows on
To neighbouring tree and leaves the distant crow
While small birds nestle in the hedge below.

JOHN CLARE

Empty Nest

Dear child, the house pines when you leave.
I research whether there is any bird who grieves
over its empty nest.

                    Your vacant room
is a still-life framed by the unclosed door;
read by sunlight, an open book on the floor.

I fold the laundry; hang your flower dress
in darkness. Forget-me-nots.

                          *

Beyond the tall fence, I hear horse-chestnuts
counting themselves.
                    Then autumn; Christmas.
You come and go, singing. Then ice; snowdrops.

Our home hides its face in hands of silence.

I knew mothering, but not this other thing
which hefts my heart each day. Heavier.
Now I know.

                          *

This is the shy sorrow. It will not speak up.

2

I play one chord on the piano;
                              it vanishes, tactful,
as dusk muffles the garden; a magpie staring from its branch.
The marble girl standing by the bench.

From the local church, bells like a spelling.
And the evening star like a text.
And then what next . . .

CAROL ANN DUFFY

Walking Away

(for Sean)

It is eighteen years ago, almost to the day –
A sunny day with the leaves just turning,
The touch-lines new-ruled – since I watched you play
Your first game of football, then, like a satellite
Wrenched from its orbit, go drifting away

Behind a scatter of boys. I can see
You walking away from me towards the school
With the pathos of a half-fledged thing set free
Into a wilderness, the gait of one
Who finds no path where the path should be.

That hesitant figure, eddying away
Like a winged seed loosened from its parent stem,
Has something I never quite grasp to convey
About nature's give-and-take – the small, the scorching
Ordeals which fire one's irresolute clay.

I have had worse partings, but none that so
Gnaws at my mind still. Perhaps it is roughly
Saying what God alone could perfectly show –
How selfhood begins with a walking away,
And love is proved in the letting go.

C. DAY LEWIS

4

For A Father

With the exact length and pace of his father's stride
The son walks,
Echoes and intonations of his father's speech
Are heard when he talks.

Once when the table was tall,
And the chair a wood,
He absorbed his father's smile and copied
The way that he stood.

He grew into exile slowly,
With pride and remorse,
In some ways better than his begetters,
In others worse.

And now having chosen, with strangers,
Half glad of his choice,
He smiles with his father's hesitant smile
And speaks with his voice.

ANTHONY CRONIN

My Brother Lives Too Far Away

My brother lives too far away
For me to see him when I would;
Which is now; is every day;
Is always, always, so I say
When I remember our boyhood.

So close together, long ago,
And he the one that knew me best;
He the one that loved me so,
Himself was nothing; this I know
Too late for my own love to rest.

It runs to tell him I have learned
At last the secret: he was I.
And still he is, though the time has turned
Us back to back, and age has burned
This difference in us till we die.

MARK VAN DOREN

To A Daughter Leaving Home

When I taught you
at eight to ride
a bicycle, loping along
beside you
as you wobbled away
on two round wheels,
my own mouth rounding
in surprise when you pulled
ahead down the curved
path of the park,
I kept waiting
for the thud
of your crash as I
sprinted to catch up,
while you grew
smaller, more breakable
with distance,
pumping, pumping
for your life, screaming
with laughter,
the hair flapping
behind you like a
handkerchief waving
goodbye.

LINDA PASTAN

Poem For My Sister

My little sister likes to try my shoes,
to strut in them,
admire her spindle-thin twelve-year-old legs
in this season's styles.
She says they fit her perfectly,
but wobbles
on their high heels, they're
hard to balance.

I like to watch my little sister
playing hopscotch,
admire the neat hops-and-skips of her,
their quick peck,
never missing their mark, not
over-stepping the line.
She is competent at peever.

I try to warn my little sister
about unsuitable shoes,
point out my own distorted feet, the calluses,
odd patches of hard skin.
I should not like to see her
in my shoes.
I wish she could stay
sure footed,
sensibly shod.

LIZ LOCHHEAD

Little Red-Cap

Mother, why have I come here? Is it
my destiny to wander this dark
forever, getting lost on the way?

Such tall trees. I cannot see
where they end, but their branches,
their hands, are rough-cast and careless

on my skin. At last now a little light is
filtering through the leaves. It draws me
like a root and by the time I emerge

I am a woman, stepping from the shadows.
Twigs snap at my feet, the forest closes
behind me. It feels my absence like a wound.

JULIA COPUS

Alice, Grown-Up,
At The Cocktail Party

The bottle still says, 'Drink me.' I still feel
All knees and elbows in a room, half hope
To shut up tidy as a telescope.
The nonsense people talk! Oh to walk out
Through a little door, into the crepusculum
Of a private garden, the only person there
Save for the nodding idiocy of flowers.
The hours pass, a slow murder of Time.
Always the golden key sits out of reach.
Always people riddle me with questions
For which there are no answers; always the wrong
Words tumble out to fill the awkward breach,
Like half-remembered lyrics from a song.
I've lost the trick of dealing packs of lies
In spades, so that the trumped heart follows suit.
The bottle says, 'Drink me.' One obeys.
If only I could forget things as they pass,
Amnesiac as the glaucous looking glass,
Or stop that sinking feeling I am falling.
Oh, to walk out the door, to where the moon
Hangs like a disembodied head's queer smile
In the branches of the trees, the curious while
Till the sun comes up and paints the roses red.

A. E. STALLINGS

The Ledge

for Alfie

Woken again by nothing, with this line
already at my back, I thought of you
at twenty, as you are – which passed somehow
while I was staring – thought how yesterday
you said you wanted to be young again,
which left me with this nothing left to say
that's woken me. You are, you are – what else
does father wail to child – though wailing it
he's woken with six-sevenths of the night
to go – you are – look I will set to work
this very moment slowing time myself,
feet to the stone and shoulder to the dark
to gain you ground – if just one ledge of light
you flutter to, right now, rereading that.

GLYN MAXWELL

Young

Loose stacks of cassettes collapse
to the slam of the door behind us.
We take the stairs
in twos and threes,

we don't know where we might be
this time next year,
but meanwhile
we apply to the future in lunch-breaks;

taste the possibility; the sweet adhesive
strip of A4 envelopes on tongues
punch the day and run
to post, to home, and out.

We eye each other up as future lovers;
our faces smooth as blank maps
of undiscovered countries,
where only we might go.

We mean to go, we thumb the guides,
we spin the globe and halt it
at Calcutta, then Alaska, now Japan,
and plan. Imagine.

Not for us the paper lanterns of remember,
but the hard bright bulbs of sheer want.
We reminisce at length
about the future, which is better;

we harbour it in our hearts
like a terrible crush. We laugh
and drink to this in rented rooms.
We think Not this, but older, elsewhere, soon.

COLETTE BRYCE

Day To Celebrate You Leaving Home

for Esther

If I could padlock today to the Millennium Bridge
I'd lock the Thames saturated in grey,
the Shard blotted in mist,
St Paul's arching over a corner of the sky;

our discussion on the difference between art and craft
on the steps of the Turbine Hall
before we climbed to the Miro,
our laughter at the gouache
'Woman with Blonde Armpit Combing Her Hair
by the Light of the Stars'
in Room 7.

I'd lock our agreement that the quickest painting
in the National Portrait Gallery Award exhibition
was the best, your choice of
black hardback notebooks, green rubber,
and clutch of bargain canvases in the shop
with its annual sale.

And you, sat at my feet in the coach station,
your hair tangled and tamed,
your navel jewel glinting
behind your black lacy top.

CHRISSIE GITTINS

Blue Girls

Twirling your blue skirts, travelling the sward
Under the towers of your seminary,
Go listen to your teachers old and contrary
Without believing a word.

Tie the white fillets then about your lustrous hair
And think no more of what will come to pass
Than bluebirds that go walking on the grass
And chattering on the air.

Practise your beauty, blue girls, before it fail;
And I will cry with my loud lips and publish
Beauty which all our power shall never establish,
It is so frail.

For I could tell you a story which is true;
I know a lady with a terrible tongue,
Blear eyes fallen from blue,
All her perfections tarnished – and yet it is not long
Since she was lovelier than any of you.

JOHN CROWE RANSOM

The Pomegranate

The only legend I have ever loved is
the story of a daughter lost in hell.
And found and rescued there.
Love and blackmail are the gist of it.
Ceres and Persephone the names.
And the best thing about the legend is
I can enter it anywhere. And have.
As a child in exile in
a city of fogs and strange consonants,
I read it first and at first I was
an exiled child in the crackling dusk of
the underworld, the stars blighted. Later
I walked out in a summer twilight
searching for my daughter at bedtime.
When she came running I was ready
to make any bargain to keep her.
I carried her back past whitebeams
and wasps and honey-scented buddleias.
But I was Ceres then and I knew
winter was in store for every leaf
on every tree in that road.
Was inescapable for each one we passed.
And for me.
                    It is winter
and the stars are hidden.
I climb the stairs and stand where I can see
my child asleep beside her teen magazines,
her can of Coke, her plate of uncut fruit . . .
The pomegranate! How did I forget it?
She could have come home and been safe
and ended the story and all

our heart-broken searching but she reached
out a hand and plucked a pomegranate.
She put out her hand and pulled down
the French sound for apple and
the noise of stone and the proof
that even in the place of death,
at the heart of legend, a child can be
hungry. I could warn her. There is still a chance.
The rain is cold. The road is flint-coloured.
The suburb has cars and cable television.
The veiled stars are above ground.
It is another world. But what else
can a mother give her daughter but such
beautiful rifts in time?
If I defer the grief I will diminish the gift.
The legend will be hers as well as mine.
She will enter it. As I have.
She will wake up. She will hold
the papery flushed skin in her hand.
And to her lips. I will say nothing.

EAVAN BOLAND

Going Out

for Eve

My daughter, heading out on the town in her glad rags,
laughs a laugh like a floribunda rose pinned in her hair.
She has so much beauty in her, more than this summer
evening, in all its frippery. More, even, than the sound
of her heels the length of the road, her phone voice
dipping into company, the pooled high talk of her
and her friends slipping through the city's open door.

Do me a favour, daughter: sometime, in time, wear for me
a sweetheart neckline, slingback sandals, my good ring
and howsoever many of your necklaces and bracelets.
Walk your walk through ten thousand doorways
so the music of you is one and the same as the music
of starlings and new moons and traffic lights and weirs,
only in a new arrangement arranged by, and for, you.

VONA GROARKE

The Buttercup Children

Down the dusty lane of summer
Thick with scent, tangled with honeysuckle,
The children come so slowly
You'd think the afternoon would lie forever
Sleeping along the hedges without shadow.

School is the past; tomorrow is only a name,
And sorrow has no share in this enchantment.
They live in the immediate delight
Of butterflies and clocks of dandelion
Blown as soon as looked at, without time
To jostle them from one thought to another.

Theirs is the present
Wide open as a daisy to the sun;
They do not bruise it in their gathering.
What though these shining buttercup bouquets
Droop in their eager hands?
The gold ungrudging petals drop behind
Uncounted through a timeless afternoon.

PHOEBE HESKETH

Outgrown

for Zoe

It is both sad and a relief to fold so carefully
her outgrown clothes and line up the little worn shoes
of childhood, so prudent, scuffed and particular.
It is both happy and horrible to send them galloping
back tappity-tap along the misty chill path into the past.

It is both freedom and a prison, to be outgrown
by her as she towers over me as thin as a sequin
in her doc martens and her pretty skirt,
because just as I work out how to be a mother
she stops being a child.

PENELOPE SHUTTLE

Demeter Mourning

Nothing can console me. You may bring silk
to make skin sigh, dispense yellow roses
in the manner of ripened dignitaries.
You can tell me repeatedly
I am unbearable (and I know this):
still, nothing turns the gold to corn,
nothing is sweet to the tooth crushing in.

I'll not ask for the impossible;
one learns to walk by walking.
In time I'll forget the empty brimming,
I may laugh again at
a bird, perhaps, chucking the nest –
but it will not be happiness,
for I have known that.

RITA DOVE

Nothing Gold Can Stay

Nature's first green is gold,
Her hardest hue to hold.
Her early leaf's a flower;
But only so an hour.
Then leaf subsides to leaf,
So Eden sank to grief,
So dawn goes down to day,
Nothing gold can stay.

ROBERT FROST

You are old, Father William

'You are old, Father William,' the young man said,
'And your hair has become very white;
And yet you incessantly stand on your head—
Do you think, at your age, it is right?'

'In my youth,' Father William replied to his son,
'I feared it might injure the brain;
But, now that I'm perfectly sure I have none,
Why, I do it again and again.'

'You are old,' said the youth, 'as I mentioned before,
And have grown most uncommonly fat;
Yet you turned a back-somersault in at the door—
Pray, what is the reason of that?'

'In my youth,' said the sage, as he shook his grey locks,
'I kept all my limbs very supple
By the use of this ointment – one shilling the box—
Allow me to sell you a couple?'

'You are old,' said the youth, 'and your jaws are too weak
For anything tougher than suet;
Yet you finished the goose, with the bones and the beak—
Pray, how did you manage to do it?'

'In my youth,' said his father, 'I took to the law,
And argued each case with my wife;
And the muscular strength, which it gave to my jaw,
Has lasted the rest of my life.'

'You are old,' said the youth, 'one would hardly suppose
That your eye was as steady as ever;
Yet you balanced an eel on the end of your nose—
What made you so awfully clever?'

'I have answered three questions, and that is enough,'
Said his father; 'don't give yourself airs!
Do you think I can listen all day to such stuff?
Be off, or I'll kick you down stairs!'

LEWIS CARROLL

One Art

The art of losing isn't hard to master;
so many things seem filled with the intent
to be lost that their loss is no disaster.

Lose something every day. Accept the fluster
of lost door keys, the hour badly spent.
The art of losing isn't hard to master.

Then practise losing farther, losing faster –
places, and names, and where it was you meant
to travel. None of these will bring disaster.

I lost my mother's watch. And look! my last, or
next-to-last, of three loved houses went.
The art of losing isn't hard to master.

I lost two cities, lovely ones. And, vaster,
some realms I owned, two rivers, a continent.
I miss them, but it wasn't a disaster.

Even losing you (the joking voice, a gesture
I love) I shan't have lied. It's evident
the art of losing's not too hard to master
though it may look like (*Write it!*) like disaster.

ELIZABETH BISHOP

Separation

Your absence has gone through me
Like thread through a needle.
Everything I do is stitched with its colour.

W. S. MERWIN

Waving Goodbye

I wanted to know what it was like before we
had voices and before we had bare fingers and before we
had minds to move us through our actions
and tears to help us over our feelings,
so I drove my daughter through the snow to meet her friend
and filled her car with suitcases and hugged her
as an animal would, pressing my forehead against her,
walking in circles, moaning, touching her cheek,
and turned my head after them as an animal would,
watching helplessly as they drove over the ruts,
her smiling face and her small hand just visible
over the giant pillows and coat hangers
as they made their turn into the empty highway.

GERALD STERN

Marigolds, 1960

You are dying. Why do we fight?
You find my first published poem –
'Not worth the paper it's printed on,'
You say. *She gave him marigolds –*

You are dying. 'They've cut out my
Wheeesht – I have to sit down
To *wheeesht* – like a woman –
Marigolds *the colour of autumn.*

I need to hitchhike to Dublin
For Trinity Term. 'I'll take you
Part of the way,' you say,
'And we can talk if you like.'

And we talk and talk as though
We know we are just in time.
'A little bit further,' you say
Again and again, and in pain.

A few miles from Drogheda
You turn the car. We say goodbye
And you drive away slowly
Towards Belfast and your death.

To keep in his cold room. Look
At me now on the Newry Road
Standing beside my rucksack. Och,
Daddy, look in your driving mirror.

MICHAEL LONGLEY

Clutch

Our kitchen door still has creaky hinges
when it's shouldered. I made a mental note
to oil it when you'd gone but the thing is
it always makes me see you in the coat
you wore the day you went away. Navy blue.
The heavy case you heaved across the jamb,
full of clothes, books and emptiness, made new
for me again that *Silver Cross*, your pram.
You filled the boot. I sat behind the wheel,
wondering if I'd ever passed my test.
Beside me in the car, you seemed to feel
the same as I did. Hoping for the best,
I trusted in a universal joint
as I let the clutch in, felt the biting point.

MICHAEL WOODS

Boy Running

for Ioan

The canal tilts him back and fore
like a boat in a toy pen
or the bubble in a spirit-level
that never quite finds its middle.
There are worse ways to grow tall
under the rustling sun and rain
between bridges 14 and 21

to outlive an owl, a drake, a hawk
where no two leaves blow the same way
and pumpkin lanterns moor for the night.

Run, boy running, run
past the sighing old man
and his blind Labrador,
the foal in her wire necklace.

Run, between east and west,
spring and autumn, dawn and dusk.
Is it your breath now or mine
deep inside your chest?

There are worse ways to never settle
in full flight, to be loved.
Run, my shadow, run.
Run but always stay in sight.

An owl cries, deep inside the trees.
The canal's glass is full of moonlight.

PAUL HENRY

Midsummer, Tobago

Broad sun-stoned beaches.

White heat.
A green river.

A bridge,
scorched yellow palms

from the summer-sleeping house
drowsing through August.

Days I have held,
days I have lost,

days that outgrow, like daughters,
my harbouring arms.

DEREK WALCOTT

February – Not Everywhere

Such days, when trees run downwind,
their arms stretched before them.

Such days, when the sun's in a drawer
and the drawer is locked.

When the meadow is dead, is a carpet
thin and shabby, with no pattern

and at bus stops people retract into collars
their faces like fists.

– And when, in a fire lit room, a mother looks
at her four seasons, her little boy

in the centre of everything, with still pools
of shadows and a fire throwing flowers.

NORMAN MACCAIG

Piano

Softly, in the dusk, a woman is singing to me;
Taking me back down the vista of years, till I see
A child, sitting under the piano, in the boom of the tingling strings
And pressing the small, poised feet of a mother who smiles as she sings.

In spite of myself, the insidious mastery of song
Betrays me back, till the heart of me weeps to belong
To the old Sunday evenings at home, with winter outside
And hymns in the cosy parlour, the tinkling piano our guide.

So now it is vain for the singer to burst into clamour
With the great black piano appassionato. The glamour
Of childish days is upon me, my manhood is cast
Down in the flood of remembrance. I weep like a child for the past.

D. H. LAWRENCE

Piano 4pm

The music lifts – up and up and up –
my son's scales,
trails his long brown fingers.

It is so particular. Doh ray mi.
He sits like time held still
on the red piano stool

Fah soh la. The scales linger on his shoulders,
circle his childhood, ti doh,
and saunter down the hall,

to float above me,
in the kitchen cooking his dinner.
The music mingles with the smells.

Biding time; holding the moment well.
In the interval, the strange space
between notes,

I chop onions. I stir and wait.
Taste and pause. I grind some pepper.
Sprinkle some sea salt. He plays Friday.

And in they come, the children
from another time; lifting their skirts, running
by the dark river.

And the bells of the past, they ring and ring,
an old woman remembers how she used to dance,
waltzing, waltzing into the night air.

And the night waves rise and crash and falter.
And the rocks are always bare and glistening.
My son plays Arioso in F

away into the future.
I can hear him grow up,
up and off, off and up.

I can see us
in the space between the bars;
mother and son.

Here we come and go.
My boy will become a man.
The light will seek the dark.

The music, majestic,
sweeps and turns,
rising and falling, innocent and knowing.

Pushing out its long limbs.
The dance the bones.
It yearns and swings

through the heart of our home.
I hold my wooden spoon mid-air,
like a proud conductor.

Tears fall down my face like notes.

JACKIE KAY

Let Him Not Grow Up

   May my little boy
stay just as he is.
He didn't suckle my milk
in order to grow up.
A child's not an oak
or a ceiba tree.
Poplars, meadow grasses,
things like that grow tall.
My little boy
can stay a mallow-flower.

   He has all he needs,
laughter, frowns, skills,
airs and graces.
He doesn't need to grow.

   If he grows they'll all come
winking at him,
worthless women
making him shameless,
or all the big boys
that come by the house.
Let my little boy
see no monsters coming.

   May his five summers
be all he knows.
Just as he is
he can dance and be happy.
May his birthdays fit
in the length of a yardstick,

all his Easters
and his Christmas Eves.

    Silly women,
don't cry. Listen:
the Sun and the stones
are born and don't grow,
they never get older,
they last forever.
In the sheepfold
kids and lambs
grow up and die:
be damned to them!

O my Lord, stop him,
make him stop growing!
Stop him and save him –
Don't let my son die!

GABRIELA MISTRAL,
translated from the Spanish by **URSULA LEGUIN**

from Book of Matches

Mother, any distance greater than single span
requires a second pair of hands.
You come to help me measure windows, pelmets, doors,
the acres of the walls, the prairies of the floors.

You at the zero-end, me with the spool of tape, recording
length, reporting metres, centimetres back to base, then leaving
up the stairs, the line still feeding out, unreeling
years between us. Anchor. Kite.

I space-walk through the empty bedrooms, climb
the ladder to the loft, to breaking point, where something
has to give;
two floors below your fingertips still pinch
the last one-hundredth of an inch . . . I reach
towards a hatch that opens on an endless sky
to fall or fly.

SIMON ARMITAGE

Freight

I am the ship in which you sail,
little dancing bones,
your passage between the dream
and the waking dream,
your sieve, your pea-green boat.
I'll pay whatever toll your ferry needs.
And you, whose history's already charted
in a rope of cells, be tender to
those other unnamed vessels
who will surprise you one day,
tug-tugging, irresistible,
and float you out beyond your depth,
where you'll look down, puzzled, amazed.

MAURA DOOLEY

My Son Stepping Out

My eye draws every line of you,
from the roots of your John Lennon mane
to the tips of your toe-tapping feet,
dressed for the high school ball
in your Grandad's white tuxedo.

The season's first snowflake
alights on your cheek as you
throw us a wave at the gate.

I tell you this,
and no mistake,
were I a girl again
on the dance floor tonight –
I know which choice I'd make.

GERDA STEVENSON

Gap Year

for Mateo

I

I remember your Moses basket before you were born.
I'd stare at the fleecy white sheet for days, weeks,
willing you to arrive, hardly able to believe
I would ever have a real baby to put in the basket.

I'd feel the mound of my tight tub of a stomach
and you moving there, foot against my heart,
elbow in my ribcage, turning, burping, awake, asleep.
One time I imagined I felt you laugh.

I'd play you Handel's Water Music or Emma Kirkby
singing Pergolesi. I'd talk to you, my close stranger,
call you Tumshie, ask when you were coming to meet me.
You arrived late, the very hot summer of eighty-eight.

You had passed the due date string of eights,
and were pulled out with forceps, blue, floury,
on the fourteenth of August on Sunday afternoon.
I took you home on Monday and lay you in your basket.

II

Now I peek in your room and stare at your bed,
hardly able to imagine you back in there sleeping.
Your handsome face – soft, open. Now you are eighteen,
six foot two, away in Costa Rica, Peru, Bolivia.

41

I follow your trails on my Times Atlas:
from the Caribbean side of Costa Rica to the Pacific,
the baby turtles to the massive leatherbacks.
Then on to Lima, to Cuzco. Your grandfather

rings: 'Have you considered altitude sickness,
Christ, he's sixteen thousand feet above sea level.'
Then to the lost city of the Incas, Macchu Picchu,
where you take a photograph of yourself with the statue

of the original Tupac. You are wearing a Peruvian hat.
Yesterday in Puno before catching the bus to Copacabana,
you suddenly appear on a webcam and blow me a kiss.
You have a new haircut; your face is grainy, blurry.

Seeing you, shy, smiling, on the webcam reminds me
of the second scan at twenty weeks, how at that fuzzy
moment back then, you were lying cross-legged with
an index finger resting sophisticatedly on one cheek.

You started the Inca trail in Arctic conditions
and ended up in subtropical. Now you plan the Amazon
in Bolivia. Your grandfather rings again to say
'There's three warring factions in Bolivia, warn him

against it. He canny see everything. Tell him to come home.'
But you say all the travellers you meet rave about Bolivia.
You want to see the Salar de Uyuni,
the world's largest salt-flats, the Amazonian rainforest.

And now you are not coming home till four weeks after
your due date. After Bolivia, you plan to stay
with a friend's Auntie in Argentina.
Then – to Chile where you'll stay with friends of Diane's.

And maybe work for the Victor Jara Foundation.
I feel like a home-alone mother; all the lights
have gone out in the hall, and now I am
wearing your large black slippers, flip-flopping

into your empty bedroom, trying to imagine you
in your bed. I stare at the photos you send by messenger:
You the top of the world, arms outstretched, eager.
Blue sky, white snow; you by Lake Tarahua, beaming.

My heart soars like the birds in your bright blue skies.
My love glows like the sunrise over the lost city.
I sing along to Ella Fitzgerald. A tisket. A tasket.
I have a son out in the big wide world.

A flip and a skip ago, you were dreaming in your basket.

JACKIE KAY

Jog On

Jog on, jog on, the footpath way,
And merrily hent the stile-a;
A merry heart goes all the day,
Your sad tires in a mile-a.

WILLIAM SHAKESPEARE

On a Son Returned to New Zealand

He is my green branch growing on a far plantation.
He is my first invention.

No one can be in two places at once.
So we left Athens on the same morning.
I was in a hot railway carriage, crammed
between Serbian soldiers and peasant
women, on sticky seats, with nothing to
drink but warm mineral water.
                              He was
in a cabin with square windows, sailing
across the Mediterranean, fast,
to Suez.
            Then I was back in London
in the tarnished summer, remembering,
as I folded his bed up, and sent the
television set away. Letters came
from Aden and Singapore, late.
                              He was
already in his father's house, on the
cliff-top, where the winter storms roll across
from Kapiti Island, and the flax bends
before the wind. He could go no further.

He is my bright sea-bird on a rocky beach.

FLEUR ADCOCK

The Lost Land

I have two daughters.

They are all I ever wanted from the earth.

Or almost all.

I also wanted one piece of ground.

One city trapped by hills. One urban river.
An Island in its element.

So I could say *mine*. *My own*.
And mean it.

Now they are grown up and far away

and memory itself
has become an emigrant,
wandering in a place
where love dissembles itself as landscape:

Where the hills
are the colour of a child's eyes,
where my children are distances, horizons:

At night,
on the edge of sleep,

I can see the shore of Dublin Bay.
Its rocky sweep and its granite pier.

Is this, I say,
how they must have seen it,
backing out on the mailboat at twilight,

shadows falling
on everything they had to leave?
And would love forever?
And then

I imagine myself
at the landward rail of that boat
searching for the last sight of a hand.

I see myself
on the underworld side of that water,
the darkness coming in fast, saying
all the names I know for a lost land:

Ireland. Absence. Daughter.

EAVAN BOLAND

Choice

I

I may raise my child in this man's house
or that man's love,
warm her on this one's smile, wean
her to that one's wit,
praise or blame at a chosen moment,
in a considered way, say
yes or no, true, false, tomorrow
not today.

Finally, who will she be
when the choices are made,
when the choosers are dead,
and of the men I love, the teeth are left
chattering with me underground?
Just the sum of me
and this or that
other?

Who can she be but, helplessly,
herself?

II

Some day your head won't find my lap
so easily. Trust is a habit you'll soon break.

Once, stroking a kitten's head
through a haze of fur, I was afraid
of my own hand, big and strong and quivering
with the urge to crush.

Here, in the neck's strong curve, the cradling arm,
love leers close to violence.

Your head too fragile, child,
under a mist of hair.
Home is the space in my lap, till the body reforms,
tissues stretch, flesh turns firm.

Your kitten-bones will Harden,
grow away from me, till you and I are sure
we are both safe.

III

I spent years hiding from your face,
the weight of your arms, warmth
of your breath. Through feverish nights,
dreaming of you, the watchdogs of virtue
and obedience crouched on my chest. *Shake
them off,* I told myself, and did. Wallowed
in small perversities, celebrated as they came
of age, matured to sins.

I call this freedom now,
watch the word cavort luxuriously, strut
my independence across whole continents
of sheets. But turning from the grasp
of arms, the rasp of breath,
to look through darkened windows at the night,
Mother, I find you staring back at me.

When did my body agree
to wear your face?

IMTIAZ DHARKER

49

Heredity

I am the family face;
Flesh perishes, I live on;
Projecting trait and trace
Through time to times anon,
And leaping from place to place
Over oblivion.

The years-heired feature that can
In curve and voice and eye
Despise the human span
Of durance – that is I;
The eternal thing in man,
That heeds no call to die.

THOMAS HARDY

Those Winter Sundays

Sundays too my father got up early
and put his clothes on in the blue black cold,
then with cracked hands that ached
from labour in the weekday weather made
banked fires blaze. No one ever thanked him.

I'd wake and hear the cold splintering, breaking.
When the rooms were warm, he'd call
and slowly I would rise and dress,
fearing the chronic angers of that house.

Speaking indifferently to him,
who had driven out the cold
and polished my good shoes as well.
What did I know, what did I know
of love's austere and lonely offices?

ROBERT HAYDEN

Parents

What it must be like to be an angel
or a squirrel, we can imagine sooner.

The last time we go to bed good,
they are there, lying about darkness.

They dandle us once too often,
these friends who become our enemies.

Suddenly one day, their juniors
are as old as we yearn to be.

They get wrinkles where it is better
smooth, odd coughs, and smells.

It is grotesque how they go on
loving us, we go on loving them.

The effrontery, barely imaginable,
of having caused us. And of how.

Their lives: surely
we can do better than that.

This goes on for a long time. Everything
they do is wrong, and the worst thing,

they all do it, is to die,
taking with them the last explanation,

how we came out of the wet sea
or wherever they got us from,

taking the last link
of that chain with them.

Father, mother, we cry, wrinkling,
to our uncomprehending children and grandchildren.

WILLIAM MEREDITH

Hedge-Jug

Cocooning us in their whisper of contact –
Calls as I carry you into the house, seven
Or six long-tailed tits flitter out of the hedge.
How can there be enough love to go round,
Conor Michael, grandson number four?
The tits build a dome with wool and moss and
Spiders' webs and feathers, then camouflage
With many lichen fragments their hedge-jug,
Feather-poke that grows as the fledglings grow.

MICHAEL LONGLEY

The Nests

for Kathryn

You ask again about the nests – the wren's
hung in the ivy above the broken pier,
a goldcrest's low in the privet,
the robin's safe in the clump of pampas.
And below the Lane Gate, coal tits
have built in the hollow post.
If you run your hand up the damp shaft
you'll find the spot, where the metal is warm.
They lead us away from the house,
under the barbed wire and down the lane to the Long Field.
We'll keep in the lee of the ditch for shelter.
Overhead a mistle-thrush stirs the hawthorn,
as out in the wind the larks have settled
in cups of grass-corn for the night.
When we cross to the Glens a snipe catapults
from the rushes close by your feet.
Now we approach the wall-dark of the wood
and hear within the wounded call of an owl.
We come in due course to a river, where I lie face down
on your surface, the rain soft on my spine.

MAURICE RIORDAN

De Profundis

Out of the deep, my child, out of the deep,
Where all that was to be, in all that was,
Whirl'd for a million aeons thro' the vast
Waste dawn of multitudinous-eddying-light –
Out of the deep, my child, out of the deep,
Thro' all this changing world of changeless law,
And every phase of ever-heightening life,
And nine long months of antenatal gloom,
With this last moon, this crescent – her dark orb
Touch'd with earth's light – thou comest, darling boy;
Our own; a babe in lineament and limb
Perfect, and prophet of the perfect man;
Whose face and form are hers and mine in one,
Indissolubly married like our love;
Live, and be happy in thyself and serve
This mortal race thy kin so well, that men
May bless thee as we bless thee, O young life
Breaking with laughter from the dark; and may
The fated channel where thy motion lives
Be prosperously shaped, and sway thy course
Along the years of haste and random youth
Unshatter'd; then full-current thro' full man;
And last in kindly curves, with gentlest fall,
By quiet fields, a slowly-dying power,
To that last deep where we and thou are still.

ALFRED, LORD TENNYSON

A Child Asleep

Angel of Words, in vain I have striven with thee,
Nor plead a lifetime's love and loyalty;
Only, with envy, bid thee watch this face,
That says so much, so flawlessly,
And in how small a space!

WALTER DE LA MARE

A Farewell

My fairest child, I have no song to give you;
No lark could pipe in skies so dull and grey;
Yet, if you will, one quiet hint I'll leave you,
For every day.

I'll tell you how to sing a clearer carol
Than lark who hails the dawn on breezy down;
To earn yourself a purer poet's laurel
Than Shakespeare's crown.

Be good, sweet maid, and let who can be clever;
Do noble things, not dream them, all day long;
And so make Life, Death and that last For Ever,
One grand sweet song.

CHARLES KINGSLEY

Song

My heart, my dove, my snail, my
  milktooth, shadow, sparrow, fingernail,
    flower-cat and blossom-hedge, mandrake

root now put to bed, moon shell, sea-swell,
  manatee, emerald shining back at me,
    nutmeg, quince, tea leaf and bone, zither,

cymbal, xylophone; paper, scissors, then
  there's stone – Who doesn't come through the door
    to get home?

CYNTHIA ZARIN

Daughter Song

for Isla

once all this is done –
soaping you in the bath
your half-songs and wet arms
and the owl in the woods behind the house
and the scream of a vole caught up
soaring through the boundless dark

and once all this is gone –
the sea crept in from the dazzling bay
its mouth even now at the red cliffs
once it's travelled in
and these high meadows are under water entirely
the vetch rotted back

and the warrens flooded sumps
and the fox runs trampled by the current
and the fox herself long drowned
still my love for you will ride, ride on
like that star in the old songs
its long-journeyed light

helpless and absolute

FIONA BENSON

If I Should Ever By Chance

If I should ever by chance grow rich
I'll buy Codham, Cockridden, and Childerditch,
Roses, Pyrgo, and Lapwater,
And let them all to my elder daughter.
The rent I shall ask of her will be only
Each year's first violets, white and lonely,
The first primroses and orchises –
She must find them before I do, that is.
But if she finds a blossom on furze
Without rent they shall be hers,
Whenever I am sufficiently rich:
Codham, Cockridden, and Childerditch,
Roses, Pyrgo and Lapwater –
I shall give them all to my elder daughter.

EDWARD THOMAS

A Kite for Michael and Christopher

All through that Sunday afternoon
a kite flew above Sunday,
a tightened drumhead, an armful of blown chaff.

I'd seen it grey and slippy in the making;
I'd tapped it when it dried out white and stiff,
I'd tied the bows of newspaper
along its six-foot tail.

But now it was far up like a small black lark
and now it dragged as if the bellied string
were a wet rope hauled upon
to lift a shoal.

My friend says that the human soul
is about the weight of a snipe
yet the soul at anchor there,
the string that sags and ascends,
weighs like a furrow assumed into the heavens.

Before the kite plunges down into the wood
and this line goes useless
take it in your two hands, boys, and feel
the strumming, rooted, long-tailed pull of grief.
You were born fit for it.
Stand in here in front of me
and take the strain.

SEAMUS HEANEY

from Leaves

V

The wood is the spring and the fire is the summer.
And the earth is our late, long summer.
Ore brings autumn, winter bears water.
We are the watering wood.

Your house was built before you were born.
The earth was yours before you were your mother's.
But it was not prepared, and its depth was not measured
and no one has said how long it should be.
Now someone shall bring you to where you must go.
Now you shall be measured and, after you, the earth.

A red buck swam in the cold pen
and breached the bank ten yards ahead,
his hot flank steaming from the sharp lake.
He was a wonder of intimidation,
all muscle and sinew and territorial pull.
I took the ground between him and your pram
certain he would run us through;
but chill had placed a tremor in his knee:
I stepped to him, he turned at heel.

Round and round the deer and the hound
where nothing is lost but sent to ground.

> Maybe it would be better to be a baby
> so you didn't have to know.

A tree on earth shall lose its leaves.
But the wood that held us holds us,
and the moment we stood in is standing.
So the wood, now, is not the wood then,
advancing like a tireless queen,
its roof of new hours and axes.
And the wood, then, is not the wood now,
but a hearth of continuous elsewhere.
A heap of earth, a slipped balloon,
hot prints lifting off the warm stone,
kicking through leaves, a callable common,
in one place and in two.

Somewhere ahead of where we are we are.
Somewhere behind of where we are we also are.
I was there with you now. I am here with you then.
The park gates close to reopen.

What domineers diminishes.
What destroys will injure the destroyer.
By earth we see earth by water water.

A power over horses and the running of the deer.
When the doorway darkens and the waves won't listen.
And the oak knight and the holly knight duel.

        Don't leave me wherever you go.
And we won't and we won't, until.

We can never go back to the watering wood.
We go back.

MATTHEW HOLLIS

The Black Guitar

Clearing out ten years from a wardrobe
I opened its lid and saw *Joe*
written twice in its dust, in a child's hand,
then a squiggled seagull or two.

      Joe, Joe,
a man's tears are worth nothing,
but a child's name in the dust, or in the sand
of a darkening beach, that's a life's work.

I touched the strings, to hear how much
two lives can slip out of tune

      then I left it,
brought down the night on it, for fear, Joe,
of hearing your unbroken voice, or the sea
as I played it.

PAUL HENRY

The Snow Man

One must have a mind of winter
To regard the frost and the boughs
Of the pine-trees crusted with snow;

And have been cold a long time
To behold the junipers shagged with ice,
The spruces rough in the distant glitter

Of the January sun; and not to think
Of any misery in the sound of the wind,
In the sound of a few leaves,

Which is the sound of the land
Full of the same wind
That is blowing in the same bare place

For the listener, who listens in the snow,
And, nothing himself, beholds
Nothing that is not there and the nothing that is.

WALLACE STEVENS

For a Lost Child

What happens is, the kind of snow that sweeps
Wyoming comes down while I'm asleep. Dawn
finds our sleeping bag but you are gone.
Nowhere now, you call through every storm,
a voice that wanders without a home.

Across bridges that used to find a shore
you pass, and along shadows of trees that fell
before you were born. You are a memory
too strong to leave this world that slips away
even as its precious time goes on.

I glimpse you often, faithful to every country
we ever found, a bright shadow the sun
forgot one day. On a map of Spain
I find your note left from a trip that year
our family travelled: 'Daddy, we could meet here.'

WILLIAM STAFFORD

Elegy for a Stillborn Child

I

Your mother walks light as an empty creel
Unlearning the intimate nudge and pull

Your trussed-up weight of seed-flesh and bone-curd
Had insisted on. That evicted world

Contracts round its history, its scar.
Doomsday struck when your collapsed sphere

Extinguished itself in our atmosphere,
Your mother heavy with the lightness in her.

II

For six months you stayed cartographer
Charting my friend from husband to father.

He guessed a globe behind your steady mound.
Then the pole fell, shooting star, into the ground.

III

On lonely journeys I think of it all,
Birth of death, exhumation for burial,

A wreath of small clothes, a memorial pram,
And parents reaching for a phantom limb.

I drive by remote control on this bare road
Under a drizzling sky, a circling rook,

Past mountain fields, full to the brim with cloud,
White waves riding home on a wintry lough.

SEAMUS HEANEY

To Our Miscarried One,
Age Thirty Now

Though I never saw you, only your clouds,
I was afraid of you, of how you differed
from what we had wanted you to be. And it's as if
you waited then, where such waiting is done,
for when I would look beside me – and here
you are, in the world of forms, where my wifehood
is now, and every action with him,
as if a thousand years from now
you and I are in some antechamber
where the difference between us is of little matter,
you with perhaps not much of a head yet,
dear garden one, you among the shovels
and spades and wafts of beekeeper's shroud
and sky-blue kidskin gloves.
That he left me is not much, compared
to your leaving the earth – your shifting places
on it, and shifting shapes – you threw off your
working clothes of arms and legs,
and moved house, from uterus
to toilet bowl and jointed stem
and sewer out to float the rivers and
bays in painless pieces. And yet
the idea of you has come back to where
I could see you today as a small, impromptu
god of the partial. When I leave for good,
would you hold me in your blue mitt
for the departure hence. I never thought
to see you again. I never thought to seek you.

SHARON OLDS

the lost baby poem

the time i dropped your almost body down
down to meet the waters under the city
and run one with the sewage into the sea
what did i know about waters rushing back
what did i know about drowning
or being drowned

you would have been born into winter
in the year of the disconnected gas
and no car   we would have made the thin
walk over Genesee hill into the Canada wind
to watch you slip like ice into strangers' hands
you would have fallen naked as snow into winter
if you were here i could tell you these
and some other things

if i am ever less than a mountain
for your definite brothers and sisters
let the rivers pour over my head
let the sea take me for a spiller
of seas   let black men call me stranger
always   for your never named sake

LUCILLE CLIFTON

from Say Something Back

XV

The flaws in suicide are clear
Apart from causing bother
To those alive who hold us dear
We could miss one another
We might be trapped eternally
Oblivious to each other
One crying *Where are you, my child*
The other calling *Mother.*

DENISE RILEY

from King John

Grief fills the room up of my absent child,
Lies in his bed, walks up and down with me,
Puts on his pretty looks, repeats his words,
Remembers me of all his gracious parts,
Stuffs out his vacant garments with his form;
Then have I reason to be fond of grief.
Fare you well. Had you such loss as I,
I could give better comfort than you do.
I will not keep this form upon my head
When there is such disorder in my wit.
O Lord, my boy, my Arthur, my fair son,
My life, my joy, my food, my all the world,
My widow-comfort, and my sorrow's cure!

WILLIAM SHAKESPEARE

A Threshold

Where have you gone, my little saving grace?
Iona or Iola of the laugh
like falling silver . . . Now nothing's in its place,
and all's as light and cold as that blue scarf
I lost or left without, or I don't own.
Everything shames me. Every card declined.
You slid between the stalls and you were gone
though I scoured the field for hours, hoping to find
you sat with 'the silent children of the fair'
or some such nonsense, though I always knew
you'd taken another hand, the way kids do,
not looking up. This place again. It's where
I wake up and recall I have no daughter
or fall asleep and dream I have no daughter.

DON PATERSON

April

Brave things are happening
    In the garden when I'm not looking.

The junction of each branch
    holds its sobriety.

Frost no longer attempts to fasten
    onto the deepest roots,

but still I'm not sure about trusting
    myself with the distances.

In the house, they come to terms.
    The youngest has gone;

the rooms vibrate, my father weighs
    his son's glasses in his hands.

The word they use for *zero* is *shunya*.
    They come to terms with its blank centre.

MONA ARSHI

The Necessity for Irony

On Sundays,
when the rain held off,
after lunch or later,
I would go with my twelve-year-old
daughter into town,
and put down the time
at junk sales, antique fairs.

There I would
lean over tables,
absorbed by
lace, wooden frames,
glass. My daughter stood
at the other end of the room,
her flame-coloured hair
obvious whenever –
which was not often –

I turned around.
I turned around.
She was gone.
Grown. No longer ready
to come with me, whenever
a dry Sunday
held out its promises
of small histories. Endings.

When I was young
I studied styles: their use
and origin. Which age
was known for which

ornament and was always drawn
to a lyric speech, a civil tone.
But never thought
I would have the need,
as I do now, for a darker one.

Spirit of irony,
my caustic author
of the past, of memory –
and of its pain, which returns
hurts stings – reproach me now,
remind me
that I was in those rooms,
with my child,
with my back turned to her,
Searching – oh irony! –
for beautiful things.

EAVAN BOLAND

Seeing the Bones

This year again the bruise-coloured oak
hangs on eating my heart out
with its slow change, the leaves at last
spiralling end over end like your
letters home that fall Fridays
in the box at the foot of the hill
saying the old news, keeping it neutral.
You ask about the dog, fourteen years
your hero, deaf now as a turnip,
thin as kindling.

In junior high your biology class
boiled a chicken down into its bones
four days at a simmer in my pot,
then wired joint by joint
the re-created hen
in an anatomy project
you stayed home from, sick.

Thus am I afflicted, seeing the bones.
How many seasons walking
on fallen apples like pebbles in
the shoes of the Canterbury faithful
have I kept the garden up
with leaves of wood ash, kitchen leavings
and the sure reciprocation of horse dung?

How many seasons have the foals
come right or breeched or in good time
turned yearlings, two-year-olds, and at three
clattered off in a ferment to the sales?

Your ponies, those dapple-grey kings
of the orchard, long gone to skeleton,
gallop across the landscape of my dreams.
I meet my father there, dead years before
you left us for a European career.
He is looping the loop on a roller coaster
called Mercy, he is calling his children in.

I do the same things day by day.
They steady me against the wrong turn,
the closed-ward babel of anomie.
This Friday your letter in thinnest blue
script alarms me. Weekly you grow
more British with your *I shalls*
and now you're off to Africa
or Everest, daughter of the file drawer,
citizen of no return. I give
your britches, long outgrown, to the crows,
your boots with a summer visit's worth
of mud caked on them to the shrews
for nests if they will have them.

Working backward I reconstruct
you. Send me your baby teeth, some new
nail parings and a hank of hair
and let me do the rest. I'll
set the pot to boil.

MAXINE KUMIN

Beattie Is Three .

At the top of the stairs
I ask for her hand. O.K.
She gives it to me.
How her fist fits my palm,
A bunch of consolation.
We take our time
Down the steep carpetway
As I wish silently
That the stairs were endless.

ADRIAN MITCHELL

To My Daughter

Bright clasp of her whole hand around my finger,
My daughter, as we walk together now.
All my life I'll feel a ring invisibly
Circle this bone with shining when she is grown
Far from today as her eyes are already.

STEPHEN SPENDER

Catrin

I can remember you, child,
As I stood in a hot, white
Room at the window watching
The people and cars taking
Turn at the traffic lights.
I can remember you, our first
Fierce confrontation, the tight
Red rope of love which we both
Fought over. It was a square
Environmental blank, disinfected
Of paintings or toys. I wrote
All over the walls with my
Words, coloured the clean squares
With the wild, tender circles
Of our struggle to become
Separate. We want, we shouted,
To be two, to be ourselves.

Neither won nor lost the struggle
In the glass tank clouded with feelings
Which changed us both. Still I am fighting
You off, as you stand there
With your straight, strong, long
Brown hair and your rosy,
Defiant glare, bringing up
From the heart's pool that old rope,
Tightening about my life,
Trailing love and conflict,
As you ask may you skate
In the dark, for one more hour.

GILLIAN CLARKE

The Malarkey

Why did you tell them to be quiet
and sit up straight until you came back?
The malarkey would have led you to them.

You go from one parked car to another
and peer through the misted windows
before checking the registration.

Your pocket bulges. You've bought them sweets
but the mist is on the inside of the windows.
How many children are breathing?

The malarkey's over in the back of the car.
The day is over outside the windows.
No streetlight has come on.

You fed them cockles soused in vinegar,
you took them on the machines.
You looked away just once.

You looked away just once
as you leaned on the chip-shop counter,
and forty years were gone.

You have been telling them for ever
Stop that malarkey in the back there!
Now they have gone and done it.
Is that mist, or water with breath in it?

HELEN DUNMORE

My Mother Said

My mother said I never should
Play with gypsies in the wood.

If I did, then she would say:
'Naughty girl to disobey!'

'Your hair shan't curl and your shoes shan't shine,
You gypsy girl, you shan't be mine!'

And my father said that if I did,
He'd rap my head with the teapot-lid.

My mother said that I never should
Play with the gypsies in the wood.

The wood was dark, the grass was green;
By came Sally with a tambourine.

I went to sea – no ship to get across;
I paid ten shillings for a blind white horse.

I upped on his back and was off in a crack.
Sally tell my mother I shall never come back.

ANONYMOUS

My Hat

Mother said if I wore this hat
I should be certain to get off with the right sort of chap
Well look where I am now, on a desert island
With so far as I can see no one at all on hand
I know what has happened though I suppose Mother wouldn't see
This hat being so strong has completely run away with me
I had the feeling it was beginning to happen the moment I put it on
What a moment that was as I rose up, I rose up like a flying swan
As strong as a swan too, why see how far my hat has flown me away
It took us a night to come and then a night and a day
And all the time the swan wing in my hat waved beautifully
Ah, I thought, How this hat becomes me
First the sea was dark then it was pale blue
And still the wing beat and we flew and we flew
A night and a day and a night, and by the old right way
Between the sun and the moon we flew until morning day.
It is always early morning here on this peculiar island
The green grass grows into the sea on the dipping land
Am I glad I am here? Yes, well I am,
It's nice to be rid of Father, Mother and the young man
There's just one thing causes me a twinge of pain,
If I take my hat off shall I find myself home again?
So in this early morning land I always wear my hat
Go home, you see, well I wouldn't run a risk like that.

STEVIE SMITH

My Complicated Daughter

What can I do for my complicated daughter,
my terror, my dark heart, so lost in this house?
Where can we meet? On the stairs, on the landing?
At night as we dream? In the bold brass of the day?
If only I could make her a cagoule of rescue,
heal all her scars, wrap her sore life in silk,
or bury her pain at the end of the garden
with my bare hands. I'd give her a sack full of wishes.
But she will not hear me, and I cannot see her.
We collide in the bathroom, by the terrible mirror,
so apart, so unable to give or receive.

JULIA DARLING

To His Son

Three things there be that prosper up apace
And flourish, whilst they grow asunder far,
But on a day, they meet all in one place,
And when they meet, they one another mar;
And they be these: the wood, the weed, the wag.
The wood is that which makes the gallow tree;
The weed is that which strings the hangman's bag;
The wag, my pretty knave, betokeneth thee.
Mark well, dear boy, whilst these assemble not,
Green springs the tree, hemp grows, the wag is wild,
But when they meet, it makes the timber rot;
It frets the halter, and it chokes the child.
Then bless thee, and beware, and let us pray
We part not with thee at this meeting day.

SIR WALTER RALEIGH

The Word

I couldn't tell you now what possessed me
to shut the summer out and stay in my room.
Or at least attempt to. In bed mostly.
It's my dad, standing in the door frame
not entering – but pausing to shape advice
that keeps coming back. 'Whatever is matter,

must *enjoy the life*.' He pronounced this twice.
And me, I heard wrongness in putting a *the*

before *life*. In two minds. Ashamed. Aware.
That I knew better, though was stuck inside
while the sun was out. That I'm native here.
In a halfway house. Like that sticking word.
That definite article, half right, half
wrong, still present between *enjoy* and *life*.

ZAFFAR KUNIAL

My Mother's Lips

Until I asked her to stop doing it and was astonished to find that
        she not only could
but from the moment I asked her in fact would stop doing it, my
        mother, all through my childhood,
when I was saying something to her, something important, would
        move her lips as I was speaking
so that she seemed to be saying under her breath the very words
        I was saying as I was saying them.

Or, even more disconcertingly – wildly so now that my puberty
        had erupted – *before* I said them.
When I was smaller, I must just have assumed that she was
        omniscient. Why not?
She knew everything else – when I was tired, or lying; she'd know
        I was ill before I did.
I may even have thought – how could it not have come into my
        mind? – that she *caused* what I said.

All she was really doing of course was mouthing my words a split
        second after I said them myself,
but it wasn't until my own children were learning to talk that I
        really understood how,
and understood, too, the edge of anxiety in it, the wanting to bring
        you along out of the silence,
the compulsion to lift you again from those blank caverns of
        namelessness we encase.

That was long afterward, though, where I was now was just
        wanting to get her to stop,
and, considering how I brooded and raged in those days, how
        quickly my teeth were on edge,

the restraint I approached her with seems remarkable, although her
    so unprotestingly
readily taming a habit by then three children and a dozen years old
    was as much so.

It's endearing to watch us again in that long-ago dusk, facing each
    other, my mother and me.
I've just grown to her height, or just past it: there are our lips
    moving together,
now the unison suddenly breaks, I have to go on by myself, no
    maestro, no score to follow.
I wonder what finally made me take umbrage enough, or heart
    enough, to confront her?

It's not important. My cocoon at that age was already unwinding:
    the threads ravel and snarl.
When I find one again, it's that two o'clock in the morning, a grim
    hotel on the square,
the impenetrable maze of an endless city, when, really alone for the
    first time in my life,
I found myself leaning from the window, incanting in a tearing
    whisper what I thought were poems.

I'd love to know what I raved that night to the night, what those
    innocent dithyrambs were,
or to feel what so ecstatically drew me out of myself and beyond . . .
    Nothing is there though,
only the solemn piazza beneath me, the riot of dim, tiled roofs and
    impassable alleys,
my desolate bed behind me, and my voice, hoarse, and the sweet
    alien air against me like a kiss.

C. K. WILLIAMS

The Way My Mother Speaks

I say her phrases to myself
in my head
or under the shallows of my breath,
restful shapes moving.
The day and ever. The day and ever.

The train this slow evening
goes down England
browsing for the right sky,
too blue swapped for a cool grey.
For miles I have been saying
What like is it,
the way I say things when I think.
Nothing is silent. Nothing is not silent.
What like is it.

Only tonight
I am happy and sad
like a child
who stood at the edge of summer
and dipped a net
in a green, erotic pond. *The day
and ever. The day and ever.*
I am homesick, free, in love
with the way my mother speaks.

CAROL ANN DUFFY

Alone

Alone. A word that chimes like a bell
for Nones or Compline, summoning
soft shadows from a cloistered past,
memories folded in their hidden hands.

Or the thrum of a wind through the palm,
dark blades snipping sparkling scraps
from a thudding sky. The whispering spin
of a leaf still curled seed in the bough.

The golden hum in the house now they've gone,
sun shimmering the stairs, a curtain tossed
aside from the window, a drowsy rose,
laughing echoes shining in the hall.

The way their names tap-dance in my brain,
trace out the letters in silver script, whirl
into a thundering dance and then
pirouette off the screen. *Pas Seul.*

*

Young hands waving,
scarves fluttering
like the white sails of boats
racing towards horizons
that only they will reach

evening
only shadows
coming home

On your wind-chimes
I hang the letters of your name.
Each time I open the door
your name rings
in an empty room.

GABRIEL GRIFFIN

Forty-One, Alone, No Gerbil

In the strange quiet, I realise
there's no one else in the house. No bucktooth
mouth pulls at a stainless steel teat, no
hairy mammal runs on a treadmill –
Charlie is dead, the last of our children's half-children.
When our daughter found him lying in the shavings, trans-
mogrified backwards from a living body
into a bolt of rodent bread
she turned her back on early motherhood
and went on single, with nothing. Crackers,
Fluffy, Pretzel, Biscuit, Charlie,
buried on the old farm we bought
where she could know nature. Well now she knows it
and it sucks. Creatures she loved, mobile and
needy, have gone down stiff and indifferent,
she will not adopt again though she cannot
have children yet, her body like a blueprint
of the understructure for a woman's body,
so now everything stops for a while,
now I must wait many years
to hear in this house again the faint
powerful call of a young animal.

SHARON OLDS

Family

My mother has gone and bought herself a piglet
because none of us comes to visit anymore.
George has good manners and is clean in his ways:
he is courtly, thoughtful, easy to amuse.
He goes to Mass with her, and sits sweetly
while she trots up to receive. He doesn't stray.
She has made a cot for him in the kitchen
where he turns in on our old clothes cut to size.

One Sunday I call on the way to somewhere else.
She props him up beside me in the high chair
and he fixes me with those dreary dark blue eyes.
When I tell him I'm glad he's there when I can't be,
he answers 'thank you' in a voice too like my own,
then bids me sit and make myself at home.

VONA GROARKE

Tea Ceremony

There are days when I pretend
to understand my mother's grief,

as I coax her into sitting at the table
for a tea ceremony, so she might

linger on the rush of green into
glass, how the scent of leaf

dissolves both past and future
in one gulp. We drink in a serene

silence, my mother smiles a smile
that breaks my breath into laughter.

She is radiant now, lost in the kettle's
repetitive chant, her gaze fixed on

the dance of fingers between utensils.
I love my mother's joy, her reprieve

from the sorrow she adorns with
designer clothing. Some nights,

I tell her: *Go to bed.* She says: *I can't.
Can you stay?* As a child, I dreaded

her desperate need, my hand resting
on her forehead, unable to let go.

Even now, with Winnicott and Klein
as bedside reading, I can only invite her

to the table: *Look, Mother, your hands
are beautiful. Look, our tea is ready.*

MARY JEAN CHAN

Late Kick-Off

My boys are coming back to me
across the Glebelands pitches
out of the echoey underpass
leaving their childhoods behind
on the other side of the motorway

letting our ghosts play on
into the dark, the four of us
hoofing the moon high,
our heads tilted, and staggering
like drunks to catch it,
waiting for it to fall . . .
the brightest ball in the sky
lighting our way home.

They are coming back to me
taller than I imagined
and too old to warm inside my fleece.
It has been too long.
They must be cold by now.
I'll warm up the engine.

I remember when the plastic goals
they used to pack, at full-time
into sacks (and bear shoulder high
like fathers, or dead kings,
back to the club-house)
were exchanged for serious steel.
After that they needed me less
and less

but look!
They are coming back to me.
Though it was I who went away.

PAUL HENRY

Eden Rock

They are waiting for me somewhere beyond Eden Rock:
My father, twenty-five, in the same suit
Of Genuine Irish Tweed, his terrier Jack
Still two years old and trembling at his feet.

My mother, twenty-three, in a sprigged dress
Drawn at the waist, ribbon in her straw hat,
Has spread the stiff white cloth over the grass.
Her hair, the colour of wheat, takes on the light.

She pours tea from a Thermos, the milk straight
From an old H.P. sauce bottle, a screw
Of paper for a cork; slowly sets out
The same three plates, the tin cups painted blue.

The sky whitens as if lit by three suns.
My mother shades her eyes and looks my way
Over the drifted stream. My father spins
A stone along the water. Leisurely,

They beckon to me from the other bank.
I hear them call, 'See where the stream-path is!
Crossing is not as hard as you might think.'
I had not thought that it would be like this.

CHARLES CAUSLEY

Soap Suds

This brand of soap has the same smell as once in the big
House he visited when he was eight; the walls of the bathroom open
To reveal a lawn where a great yellow ball rolls back through a hoop
To rest at the head of a mallet held in the hands of a child.

And these were the joys of that house: a tower with a telescope;
Two great faded globes, one of the earth, one of the stars;
A stuffed black dog in the hall; a walled garden with bees;
A rabbit warren; a rockery; a vine under glass; the sea.

To which he has now returned. The day of course is fine
And a grown-up voice cries Play! The mallet slowly swings,
Then crack, a great gong booms from the dog-dark hall and the ball
Skims forward through the hoop and then through the next and then

Through hoops where no hoops were and each dissolves in turn
And the grass has grown head-high and an angry voice cries Play!
But the ball is lost and the mallet slipped long since from the hands
Under the running tap that are not the hands of a child.

LOUIS MACNEICE

To My Cottage

Thou lowly cottage where my first breath I drew,
Past joys endear thee, childhood's past delight
Where each young summer's pictured on my view,
And, dearer still, the happy winter-night
When the storm pelted down with all his might
And roared and bellowed in the chimney-top
And pattered vehement 'gainst the window-light
And on the threshold fell the quick eaves-drop.
How blest I've listened on my corner stool,
Heard the storm rage, and hugged my happy spot,
While the fond parent wound her whirring spool
And spared a sigh for the poor wanderer's lot.
In thee, sweet hut, this happiness was proved,
And these endear and make thee doubly loved.

JOHN CLARE

Voices

I heard those voices today again:
Voices of women and children, down in that hollow
Of blazing light into which swoops the tree-darkened lane
Before it mounts up into the shadow again.

I turned the bend – just as always before
There was no one at all down there in the sunlit hollow;
Only ferns in the wall, foxgloves by the hanging door
Of that blind old desolate cottage. And just as before

I noticed the leaping glitter of light
Where the stream runs under the lane; in that mine-dark archway
– Water and stones unseen as though in the gloom of night –
Like glittering fish slithers and leaps the light.

I waited long at the bend of the lane,
But heard only the murmuring water under the archway.
Yet I tell you, I've been to that place again and again,
And always, in summer weather, those voices are plain,
Down near that broken house, just where the tree-darkened lane
Swoops into the hollow of light before mounting to shadow again . . .

FRANCES BELLERBY

To A Young Child

Margaret, are you grieving
Over Goldengrove unleaving?
Leaves, like the things of man, you
With your fresh thoughts care for, can you?
Ah! as the heart grows older
It will come to such sights colder
By and by, nor spare a sigh
Though worlds of wanwood leafmeal lie;
And yet you *will* weep and know why.
Now no matter, child, the name:
Sorrow's springs are the same.
Nor mouth had, no nor mind, expressed
What heart heard of, ghost guessed:
It is the blight man was born for,
It is Margaret you mourn for.

GERARD MANLEY HOPKINS

Living

The fire in leaf and grass
so green it seems
each summer the last summer.

The wind blowing, the leaves
shivering in the sun,
each day the last day.

A red salamander
so cold and so
easy to catch, dreamily

moves his delicate feet
and long tail. I hold
my hand open for him to go.

Each minute the last minute.

DENISE LEVERTOV

The Red Hat

It started before Christmas. Now our son
Officially walks to school alone.
Semi-alone, it's accurate to say:
I or his father track him on the way.
He walks up on the east side of West End,
we on the west side. Glances can extend
(and do) across the street; not eye contact.
Already ties are feeling and not fact.
Straus Park is where these parallel paths part;
he goes on alone from there. The watcher's heart
stretches, elastic in its love and fear,
toward him as we see him disappear,
striding briskly. Where two weeks ago,
holding a hand, he'd dawdle, dreamy, slow,
he now is hustled forward by the pull
of something far more powerful than school.
The mornings we turn back to are no more
than forty minutes longer than before,
but they feel vastly different – flimsy, strange,
wavering in the eddies of this change,
empty, unanchored, perilously light
since the red hat vanished from our sight.

RACHEL HADAS

Conversation With Fantasy Mother

Dear fantasy mother, thank you
for taking my coming out as calmly
as a pond accepts a stone
flung into its depths.

You sieved my tears, added
an egg, then baked a beautiful cake.
You said: *Let us celebrate, for today*
you are reborn as my beloved.

The candles gleamed and the icing
was almost true – impossibly white –
coated with the sweetness of
sprinkles. We sat together

at the table and ate. Afterwards,
I returned to my room and touched
all the forbidden parts of myself, felt
a kindness I had not known in years.

MARY JEAN CHAN

God Is Dead – Nietzsche

Daddy and I are always here, you know,
Whenever you want us.
We didn't like the things you said
The last time home.
Bourgeois, you said, and a word which sounded
Very like atrophied.
Daddy doesn't like the way you collect
Toilet graffiti,
God is dead – Nietzsche, and the reply
Nietzsche is dead – God.

You can't expect Daddy to go round
With the plate in church
With thoughts like that in his head.
I worry too.
Structuralism sounds like a building-site.
Semiology sounds rather rude
In a medical kind of way.
The dogs are well, both almost human,
As we've often said
To you.

Please wear a vest, the days are getting
Colder. We hope you will not be so rude
The next time home.
Daddy and I have just re-done your room.
The blood on the wall hardly shows
After two coats of paint.
Cambridge must be very pretty just now.
I am, in spite of everything,
Your loving Mother.

ELIZABETH BARTLETT

Things My Father Told Me

The Latin for 'Do your own homework, you bastard.'
That, like a bee, a line from Virgil has six feet.

The German for 'Are those sultanas, or do you keep rabbits under
    the counter?'
King's College pinkos would sell me to the Russians.

That engineers make useful husbands. The way to check tyre
    pressure.
How to prune vines, willows and cypresses.

A method for telling if Gorms are living in your cairns.
Naismith's rule for pace and gradient.

That in his day, you hiked two hundred and sixty-seven miles
on beer and Kendal mint cake and were grateful.

Munro charted the Highlands by night, with a darkened lantern.
Wainwright loved his dogs more than his wives.

That if a Bedouin calls your mother a swine
you reply: 'Stick your head up a dead bear's arse.'

YVONNE REDDICK

from Hamlet

Give thy thoughts no tongue.
Nor any unproportioned thought his act.
Be thou familiar, but by no means vulgar.
Those friends thou hast, and their adoption tried,
Grapple them to thy soul with hoops of steel;
But do not dull thy palm with entertainment
Of each new-hatch'd, unfledged comrade. Beware
Of entrance to a quarrel, but being in
Bear't that the opposed may beware of thee.
Give every man thy ear, but few thy voice;
Take each man's censure, but reserve thy judgement.
Costly thy habit as thy purse can buy.
But not express'd in fancy rich, nor gaudy;
For the apparel oft proclaims the man,
And they in France of the best rank and station
Are of a most select and generous chief in that.
Neither a borrower nor a lender be;
For loan oft loses both itself and friend.
And borrowing dulls the edge of husbandry.
This above all: to thine own self be true,
And it must follow as the night the day
Thou canst not then be false to any man.

WILLIAM SHAKESPEARE

The Mud-Spattered Recollections of a Woman Who Lived Her Life Backwards

I'll tell you a tale: one morning as I lay
in my uncomfortable six-foot small grave,
I lay sulking about a somewhat too short-lit
life both fruitful and dutiful.

It was death it was death like an inbreath fully inhaled
in the grief of the world when at last
there began to emerge a way out, alas
the in-snowing silence made any description difficult.

No eyes no matches and yet mathematically speaking
I could still reach at a stretch a waspish whiteish
last seen outline any way up, which could well be my own
were it only a matter of refolding.

So I creased I uncreased and the next thing I knew
I was pulled from the ground at the appointed hour
and rushed to the nearest morgue to set out yet again
from the bed to the floor to the door to the air.

And there was the car still there in its last known place
under the rain where I'd left it, my husband etc.
even myself in retrospect I was still there
still driving back with the past all spread out already in front of me.

What a refreshing whiff with the windows open!
There were the dead leaves twitching and tacking back
to their roosts in the trees and all it required
was a certain minimum level of inattention.

I tell you, for many years from doorway to doorway
and in through series of rooms I barely noticed
I was humming the same tune twice. I was seeing the same
three children racing towards me getting smaller and smaller.

This tale's like a rose once opened it
cannot reclose, it continues: one morning
one terrible morning for maybe the hundredth time
they came to insert my third child back inside me.

It was death it was death: from head to foot
I heard myself crack with the effort, I leaned and cried
and a feeling fell on me with a dull clang
that I'd never see my darling daughter again.

Then both my sons, slowly at first
then faster and faster, their limbs retracted inwards
smaller and smaller till all that remained
was a little mound where I didn't quite meet in the middle.

Well either I was or was not either living or dead
in a windowless cubicle of the past, a mere
8.3 light minutes from the present moment when at last
my husband walked oh dear he walked me to church.

All in one brief winter's day, both
braced for confusion with much shy joy,
reversed our vows, unsigned our hands
and slid them back in our pockets. God knows why.

What then what then I'll tell you what then: one evening
there I stood in the matchbox world of childhood
and saw the stars fall straight through Jimmy's binoculars,
they looked so weird skewered to a fleeting instant.

Then again and again for maybe the hundredth time
they came to insert me feet first into nothing
complete with all my missing hopes – next morning
there was still that same old humming thrum still there.

That same old humming thrumming sound that is either
my tape re-winding again or maybe it's stars
passing through stars coming back to their last known places,
for as far as I know in the end both sounds are the same.

ALICE OSWALD

Whoever She Was

They see me always as a flickering figure
on a shilling screen. Not real. My hands,
still wet, sprout wooden pegs. I smell the apples
burning as I hang the washing out.
Mummy, say the little voices of the ghosts
of children on the telephone. Mummy.

A row of paper dollies. Cleaning wounds
or boiling eggs for soldiers. The chant
of magic words repeatedly. I do not know.
Perhaps tomorrow. If we're very good.
The film is on a loop. Six silly ladies
torn in half by baby fists. When they
think of me, I'm bending over them at night
to kiss. Perfume. Rustle of silk. Sleep tight.

Where does it hurt? A scrap of echo clings
to the bramble bush. My maiden name
sounds wrong. This was the playroom.
These are the photographs. Making masks
from turnips in the candlelight. In case they come.

Whoever she was, forever their wide eyes watch her
as she shapes a church and steeple in the air.
She cannot be myself and yet I have a box
of dusty presents to confirm that she was here. Telling stories
or pretending to be strong. Mummy's never wrong.
You open your dead eyes to look in the mirror
which they are holding to your mouth.

CAROL ANN DUFFY

The Envelope

It is true, Martin Heidegger, as you have written,
I fear to cease, even knowing that at the hour
of my death my daughters will absorb me, even
knowing they will carry me about forever
inside them, an arrested foetus, even as I carry
the ghost of my mother under my navel, a nervy
little androgynous person, a miracle
folded in lotus position.

Like those old pear-shaped Russian dolls that open
at the middle to reveal another and another, down
to the pea-sized, irreducible minim,
may we carry our mothers forth in our bellies.
May we, borne onward by our daughters, ride
in the Envelope of Almost Infinity,
that chain letter good for the next twenty-five
thousand days of their lives.

MAXINE KUMIN

Mirror

In my mother's house
is the friendly mirror,
the only glass in which I look
and think I see myself,
think, yes, that's what
I think I'm like,
that's who I am. The only
glass in which I look and smile.

Just as this baby smiles
at the baby who always
smiles at her, the one in
her mother's arms, the mother
who looks like me, who
smiles at herself in her
mother's mirror, the friendly
mirror in her mother's house.

But if I move to one side
we vanish, the woman I thought
was me, the baby making friends
with herself, we move to one side
and the mirror holds no future, no past,
in its liquid frame, only the corner
of an open window, a bee visiting
the ready flowers of summer.

MAURA DOOLEY

Praise Song For
My Mother

You were
water to me
deep and bold and fathoming

You were
moon's eye to me
pull and grained and mantling

You were
sunrise to me
rise and warm and steaming

You were
the fishes' red gill to me
the flame tree's spread to me
the crab's leg/ the fried plantain smell
                  replenishing replenishing

Go to your wide futures, you said

GRACE NICHOLS

Woman to Child

You who were darkness warmed my flesh
where out of darkness rose the seed.
Then all a world I made in me;
all the world you hear and see
hung upon my drawing blood.

There moved the multitudinous stars,
and coloured birds and fishes moved.
There swam the sliding continents.
All time lay rolled in me, and sense,
and love that knew not its beloved.

O node and focus of the world;
I hold you deep within that well
you shall escape and not escape –
that mirrors still your sleeping shape;
that nurtures still your crescent cell.

I wither and you break from me;
yet though you dance in living light
I am the earth, I am the root,
I am the stem that fed the fruit,
the link that joins you to the night.

JUDITH WRIGHT

December

'The end of a thing
is never the end,
something is always
being born like
a year or a baby.'

'I don't understand,'
Everett Anderson says.
'I don't understand where
the whole thing's at.'

'It's just about Love,'
his Mama smiles.
'It's all about Love and
you know about that.'

LUCILLE CLIFTON

Shard

It was late when you called to say
you were on Southwark Bridge,

waving beneath a lamppost.
Third from the left.

So I stood at the window,
fifty floors up, pinned you

with the binoculars
which came with the room

then flashed the bathroom light;
morse code.

Around you, trains eased through
boroughs on wishbone tracks;

lanterns of Londoners
headed for home.

You danced on the road, blowing kisses,
giddy with seeing me,

your daughter, blinking my small light
down on the city;

the space between us swollen
and homesick, a mile long.

ELLA DUFFY

Your Poem Here

for
from

Permission acknowledgements

The publishers are grateful to the following for permission to reproduce copyright material.

Fleur Adcock, 'On a Son Returned to New Zealand', from *Poems 1960–2000* (Bloodaxe Books, 2000).

Simon Armitage, extract from *Book of Matches* by Simon Armitage (Faber and Faber Limited).

Mona Arshi, 'April', from Small Hands (Liverpool University Press), reproduced with permission of the Licensor through PLSclear.

Elizabeth Bartlett, 'God is Dead – Nietzsche', from *Two Women Dancing: New & Selected Poems* (Bloodaxe Books, 1995).

Eavan Boland, 'The Lost Land', 'The Necessity for Irony' and 'The Pomegranate', from *New Collected Poems* (Carcanet, 2005).

Colette Bryce, 'Young', from *Selected Poems* copyright © Colette Bryce 2017.

Charles Causley, 'Eden Rock', from *Collected Poems 1951–2000* copyright © Charles Causley 1951, 1953, 1957, 1961, 1968, 1969, 1970, 1975, 1981, 1984, 1986, 1987, 1988, 1991, 1992, 1993, 1994, 1996, 1997, 2000.

Mary Jean Chan, 'Conversations with Fantasy Mother' and 'Tea Ceremony', from *Flèche* by Mary Jean Chan (Faber and Faber Limited).

Gillian Clarke, 'Catrin', from *Selected Poems* by Gillian Clarke. Published by Picador. Copyright © Gillian Clarke. Reproduced by permission of the author c/o Rogers, Coleridge & White Ltd., 20 Powis Mews, London W11 1JN.